THE QUEEN'S HANDKERCHIEF

This is the story of a little girl, a queen and a handkerchief.

This is the little girl.
Her name is Ann.

Ann's house is in a village.

It is a little village.

There are ten houses in the village.

There are two shops and there is one school.

Can you see Ann's house?

It is beside the water.

It has a blue door.

It has two windows.

They are blue too.

Behind the house is a tall tree.

In front of the house is a seat.

The seat is green.

Can you see it?

Ann's mother and father have a shop.
The shop is in the village too.

There is bread in the shop.
There are cakes in the shop.
Can you see Ann's mother and father?
They are in the shop.
Can you see Dick?
He is standing in front of the shop.
Dick is Ann's brother.

It is eight o'clock in the morning.
The sky is blue and the sun is shining.
The birds are singing.
People are working.
Ann's mother and father are working.
Dick is helping his father.
Ann is playing.

Look.
A man is coming.
He is on a horse.
The horse is black.
The man is riding a black horse.

The people are looking at the man.
'Look at his clothes,' says Dick.
'Who is it?' says Ann.
'He is the Queen's man,' says Father.
'What is he doing in the village?'

'Look,' says Ann. 'He is putting a
notice on the notice-board.'

Father is reading the notice.
'Listen,' he says.
'The Queen is coming to the village.
She is coming this afternoon.
Queen Ann is coming to this village.'

The children are shouting and clapping.
'The Queen,' says Dick.
'Queen Ann is coming to the village.'

It is nine o'clock.

The people are working.

Ann is working.

Dick is working.

They are cleaning the village.

The men are cutting the grass.

Dick is helping the men.

The women are sweeping the floors.

Ann is helping.

The teacher is writing.

She is writing a song.

It is a new song.

It is eleven o'clock.

The men are cleaning the windows.

The women are making bread.
They are making cakes.

The children are singing.
They are singing a new song.
They are singing the teacher's song.

It is twelve o'clock.

Look.

The men are carrying flowers.

There are long tables on the grass.

The women are putting white tablecloths on the tables.

They are clean tablecloths.

They are very clean and white.

The women are putting plates on the tables.

They are putting cups on the tables.

Ann is helping and Dick is helping.

It is one o'clock.
The teacher is carrying a big basket.
There are flowers in the basket.
She is talking to Ann.
'Ann,' she says. 'Give these to the Queen.
Give the flowers to Queen Ann.'

Mother is very happy.
'Go and wash,' she says to Ann.
'Wash your face. Wash your hands.
Put on your new dress and your new shoes.'
'Yes, mother,' says Ann.
'Brush your hair too,' says Mother.

It is two o'clock.
Dick is standing on the wall.
He is looking at the road.
'Can you see the Queen?'
says Father.
'No,' says Dick.

The people are waiting.
They are waiting for the Queen.
'I can see the Queen,' says Dick.
'I can see men and I can see
horses.'
'How many people are there?'
says Father.
'I can see six people,'
says Dick.
'There is the Queen and there
are five men.
I can see six horses.'
'Come, Dick,' says Father.
'Come and help.'
'Pick up the flowers, Ann,'
says Mother.

Can you see the Queen?
She is riding a white horse.
There are five men behind the Queen.
They are riding horses too.
The men's horses are black.
They are riding on black horses.

The teacher is talking to the children.
'Sing the new song,' she says.

The children are singing.
The women are throwing flowers.
They are throwing flowers in front of the Queen.
She is smiling.

'Look,' says Dick. 'A man is holding the
Queen's horse. Go, Ann.
Give the flowers to the Queen.'

Ann is running.
She is running to the Queen.
Her dress is very long.
Her red shoes are very new.

Look.
Ann is falling.

Look at Ann.
Her face is dirty.
Her hands are dirty.
Her new dress is dirty.
She is crying.

The flowers are on the road.

'Pick up the flowers,' says the Queen.

The Queen's men are picking up the flowers.

The Queen is smiling at Ann.

'Come,' says the Queen to Ann.

The Queen is talking to her men.

'Please give me a bowl of water,' she says.

The people are looking at the Queen.

'What is she doing?' says Father.

'She is washing Ann's face,' says Mother.

Ann is smiling.
Her hands are clean.
Her face is clean.
The Queen is smelling her flowers.

The Queen is talking to Ann.
'What is your name?' she says.
'It is Ann,' says Ann.

The Queen is laughing.
She is giving a handkerchief to Ann.
It is clean and white.
It is the Queen's handkerchief.
'Look at this,' says the Queen. 'This is my name.
It is your name too and it is your handkerchief.'

QUESTIONS AND EXERCISES

Page 1

  1 Who are in the story?
  2 What is the little girl's name?

Page 2

  1 Where is Ann's house?
  2 Is the village big?
  3 How many houses are there in the village?
  4 How many shops are there?
  5 Are there two schools?
  6 What colour is the door of Ann's house?
  7 What colour are the windows?
  8 *Finish this*: 'Behind the house is . . .'
  9 What is in front of the house?
10 What colour is it?

Page 3

  1 *Finish this*: 'Ann's mother and father have . . . .'
  2 Where is the shop?
  3 What is in the shop?
  4 Where are Ann's mother and father?
  5 Where is Dick standing?
  6 Who is Dick?

Page 4

  1 What time is it?
  2 What colour is the sky?
  3 What are the birds doing?

4 What are the people doing?
5 *Finish this*: 'Dick . . . his father.'
6 Is Ann working?

Page 5

1 Who is coming?
2 What is he riding?
3 What colour is it?
4 What are the people doing?
5 *Finish this*: '"He is the . . . ," says Father.'
6 Look at the second picture. Where is the man putting the notice?

Page 6

1 What is Father reading?
2 Who is coming to the village?
3 *Finish this*: 'She is coming . . . .'
4 What are the children doing?
5 Are they unhappy?

Page 7

1 What time is it?
2 Are the people working?
3 What is Ann doing?
4 Is Dick playing?
5 What are the men cutting?
6 *Finish this*: 'The women . . . the floors.'
7 What is the teacher doing?
8 Is it a new song?

20

Page 8

1 Is it ten o'clock?
2 What are the men cleaning?
3 Are the women making bread?
4 What are the children doing?
5 *Finish this*: 'They are singing . . . .'

Page 9

1 What time is it?
2 Are the men carrying tables?
3 What are on the grass?
4 What are the women putting on the tables?
5 Are they dirty tablecloths?
6 What colour are the tablecloths?
7 Are the women putting plates on the tables?
8 *Finish this*: 'They are . . . on the the tables.'
9 What are Ann and Dick doing?

Page 10

1 Is it three o'clock?
2 What is the teacher carrying?
3 What is in the basket?
4 Who is the teacher talking to?
5 *Finish this*: 'Give . . . to Queen Ann.'
6 Look at the second picture. Is Mother happy?
7 *Finish this*: 'Wash your . . . . Wash your . . . .
   Put on your new . . . and your new . . . .'

Page 11

1 What time is it?
2 What is Dick standing on?
3 What is he doing?
4 Can he see the Queen?
5 Look at the second picture. What are the people doing?
6 Who are they waiting for?
7 What can Dick see?
8 How many people can Dick see?
9 How many horses are there?
10 What is Father saying to Dick?

Page 12

1 What is the Queen riding on?
2 What colour is the Queen's horse?
3 Where are the five men?
4 What colour are the men's horses?
5 Look at the second picture. What is the
   teacher saying to the children?

Page 13

1 What are the children doing?
2 What are the women doing?
3 Are they throwing flowers behind the Queen?
4 Is she smiling?
5 Look at the second picture. What is the man holding?

Page 14

1 What is Ann doing?
2 Who is she running to?
3 Is her dress short?

4 What colour are her shoes?

5 Look at the second picture. Is Ann falling?

6 Look at the third picture. Is Ann's face clean?

7 Are her hands dirty?

8 Is her dress clean or dirty?

9 Is Ann happy?

Page 15

1 Where are the flowers?

2 What are the Queen's men doing?

3 Is the Queen smiling?

4 Look at the second picture. Who is the Queen talking to?

5 What is in the bowl?

6 Who are looking at the Queen?

7 What is the Queen doing?

Page 16

1 Is Ann smiling?

2 Are her hands dirty?

3 Is her face clean?

4 What is the Queen smelling?

5 Look at the second picture. What is the Queen doing?

6 *Finish this*: '"What is your . . . ?" she says.'

Page 17

1 Is the Queen smiling?

2 What is she giving to Ann?

3 What colour is it?

4 Is it dirty?

5 What is on the handkerchief?

6 *Finish this*: 'It is your . . . and it is . . . .'

WORDS IN THIS BOOK

afternoon

a basket

birds

black

blue

a bowl

bread

cakes

carrying

clapping

cleaning

clean

dirty

crying

cups

cutting

a door	a dress	a face	falling
a floor	flowers	give	grass
green	hair	hands	a handkerchief
happy	helping	holding	a horse

a house	laughing	listen	long
a name	new	a notice	a notice-board
people	pick up	plates	playing
queen	reading	riding	a road

running	a seat	shining	a shop
shoes	shouting	singing	sky
smelling	smiling	standing	sweeping
the sun	a table	a tablecloth	talking

a tree	a tall tree	throwing	waiting
a village		a wall	wash
water	white	windows	writing
working	behind the house	beside the house	in front of the house

Start with English Readers

Grade 1
Po-Po
Mary and her Basket
Pat and her Picture
A New Tooth
The Kite

Grade 2
Peter and his Book
John and Paul go to School
The Bird and the Bread
Two Stories
Tonk and his Friends

Grade 3
Sam's Ball
The Fox and the Stork/The Bird and the Glass
The Big Race
The Man in the Big Car
The Queen's Handkerchief

Grade 4
Nine Stories About People
Four Clever People
In the Cave
An Apple for the Monkey

Grade 5
People and Things
Doctor Know It All/The Brave Little Tailor
The Flyer

Grade 6
The Bottle Imp
The World Around Us

Start with English Readers are also available on cassette.

Start with Words and Pictures

This alphabetical picture dictionary provides extra help for Grades 1 to 3. It has been specially written for use with *Start with English* materials.

For practice using the words in the picture dictionary, there is the *Start with Words and Pictures Activity Book.*